30 Minutes ... To Improve Your Networking Skills

HILTON CATT and PATRICIA SCUDAMORE

KOGAN PAGE

First published in the UK by Kogan Page, 2000

Kogan Page Limited
120 Pentonville Road
London N1 9JN

British Library Cataloguing in Publication Data
A CIP record for this book is available from the British Library.

ISBN 0 7494 3316 7

Typeset by Florence Production Ltd, Stoodleigh, Devon
Printed and bound in Great Britain by Clays Ltd, St Ives plc

The 30 Minutes Series

Titles available are: *30 Minutes . . .*

Before a Meeting

Before a Presentation

Before Your Job Appraisal

Before Your Job Interview

To Boost Your Communication
Skills

To Boost Your Self-Esteem

To Brainstorm Great Ideas

To Deal with Difficult People

To Get Your Own Way

To Get Yourself Promoted

To Improve Telesales
Techniques

To Make the Right Decision

To Make the Right Impression

To Make Yourself Richer

To Manage Information
Overload

To Manage Your Time Better

To Market Yourself

To Master the Internet

To Motivate Your Staff

To Negotiate a Better Deal

To Plan a Project

To Prepare a Job Application

To Solve That Problem

To Succeed in Business
Writing

To Understand the Financial
Pages

To Write a Business Plan

To Write a Marketing Plan

To Write a Report

To Write Sales Letters

Available from all good booksellers.
For further information on the series, please contact:

Kogan Page, 120 Pentonville Road, London N1 9JN
Tel: 020 7278 0433 Fax: 020 7837 6348

www.kogan-page.co.uk

CONTENTS

⏰ Contents

1

PICKING THE RIGHT PEOPLE TO NETWORK WITH

Networking starts with people you know. But this isn't to say you network with everyone you know. Indeed, from a networking point of view, you need to be very careful about who you include in your circle and, as we shall see shortly, some people are best left well alone.

In setting off on this crash course in improving your networking skills, the first subject we want to look at is how to go about getting onto networking terms with the right people and, conversely, how to make sure you give the wrong people a wide berth.

PROFESSIONAL NETWORKING

This is by way of a definition before we start. The context in which we are using the term networking is that of your work. More properly, we should be referring to such networking as *professional networking* to distinguish it from the kind of networking you do with your family and friends or with those with whom you share your leisure pursuits. Different rules apply to professional networking and you should always make the distinction.

YOUR GREAT NETWORKING SUPERHIGHWAY

A useful way to consider the links in a networking relationship is to compare them to a great superhighway where the traffic is going in both directions. You network someone and they network you back. Someone does you a good turn by effecting an important introduction for you and, a few months later, they want you to do the same for them. This mutually beneficial arrangement of you scratching their back while they scratch yours is what networking is all about and it's fine of course so long as you have no misgivings about the other person. You are happy to put in a good word for them to help them get business. You have no qualms about sharing sensitive information with them. You are prepared to put your reputation on the line by recommending them for a top job.

But what if this isn't the case? What if you have doubts about John or Jenny Doe's work ethics or their personal integrity? Should you be sticking your neck out for them quite so readily?

The answer, needless to say, is no and to illustrate why let's ask Neil to tell us what happened when he found himself on the receiving end of a cry for help from his old friend Harriet.

Neil: Harriet and I go back a long way. We graduated together and we've kept in touch ever since – meeting for a drink or a game of tennis from time to time. About a month ago I received a phone call from Harriet to say she'd lost her job with the firm of management consultants where she'd been working. She blamed it on cutbacks but I had my suspicions. Harriet may be great fun but she will never win any prizes for reliability or organizing herself.

What Harriet wanted me to do, however, was to have a word with Mike, my boss, to see if he could find a slot for her with the firm. A few warning bells immediately sounded off in my head but I couldn't see any way of saying no to Harriet. After all, she'd done so many good turns for me in the past.

The upshot was that Mike offered Harriet a job. Then, on the morning she was supposed to start, she didn't turn up. Mike went ballistic – not surprisingly. He called me into the office and told me not to bother introducing any of my friends ever again, and he's been frosty with me since. As to Harriet, she'd been offered a job somewhere else on better pay. Didn't she think to let Mike know? Unfortunately not, but sadly that's Harriet all over.

NETWORKING WITH PEOPLE WHO COULD LET YOU DOWN

Neil found out the hard way that networking with people who are unsatisfactory for one reason or another usually ends in tears. But while he's contemplating how to get his relationship with Mike back on track perhaps he should be reflecting on how much worse things could have been for him if Harriet had actually joined the firm.

So what's the lesson here? Simply this – never network with anyone who could let you down because they will call in the favours from time to time and you will find it hard to refuse them. Like Neil, the result could be that your reputation suffers in quarters where it matters.

PROPRIETORSHIP OF YOUR NETWORK

Think of your network as a small business over which you have sole proprietorship rights. With your ownership comes responsibility, of course, and not least, the responsibility for hire and fire. In exercising this responsibility:

- **Be firm**. Strike anyone off your network who doesn't measure up.

- **Don't fudge**. As far as membership of your network is concerned, never be tempted to give anyone the benefit of the doubt. Don't give second chances to those who let you down. View one bad experience as enough.

- **Be flexible**. Allow for the fact that people change and sometimes for the worse. Remember that, as far as your network is concerned, there's no such thing as life membership.

PROACTIVE AND REACTIVE NETWORKING

At this juncture, let's introduce you to some terminology.

Proactive networking is the networking you instigate. If you like, it is the outbound traffic on your great networking superhighway. Proactive networking will be generated by some need you have – a need, say, for an introduction or for someone to put in a good word for you or because you need access to some information.

Reactive networking, conversely, is the networking that comes the other way (the inbound traffic). It is generated by the needs of others, needs they will see you as being able to satisfy.

Proactive and reactive networking are interdependent. One thrives on the other and this bouncing backwards and forwards of messages is the key to understanding what makes networks work.

SEVERING YOUR NETWORKING LINKS WITH PEOPLE WHO DON'T MEASURE UP

How do you do this?

If you want to close off one of your superhighways, the first step to take is to stop using it. Don't send any more traffic off down the outbound lane and you'll find the traffic coming back the other way has a natural tendency to dry up. Why? Networks need to be constantly switching from the proactive to the reactive and back again in order to thrive and without this constant switching they soon wither and die. Networking with someone effectively gives them an open invitation to network you back, but without this open invitation they will be less sure of their ground and think twice before picking up the phone. A few polite but firm cold shoulders should serve to put the final kiss of

---

TIP

Don't network with people who are awkward or who won't help. Put them on the list for de-selection straight away.

13

death on any networking relationships you no longer wish to continue with. Later in the book you'll be learning about approachability and availability. If you want to freeze someone out these are lessons you need to apply in reverse.

TAKING STOCK OF YOUR NETWORK

Having pruned out the dead wood from your network along with any parasites, it's time to cast your eyes over what's left.

Sadly, the term 'networking' is a complete turn-off for many people largely because it conjures up images of endless rounds of gossipy social gatherings of the sort they dread. First point first therefore: everyone in a career has got a professional network, whether they would choose the term or not. It could almost be described as unavoidable.

Who features on the typical professional network? A snapshot usually reveals a complete mix of people such as:

● work colleagues past and present, including bosses, peers and subordinates;

● other business contacts such as customers and suppliers;

● people you meet through going on external courses or because you belong to a professional body.

Networks also reflect the routes that careers have followed. For example, someone who has moved around a lot or worked overseas will have a very different network to someone whose experience is essentially one company.

SIZE – AND WHETHER IT MATTERS

A lot of the effort that goes into professional networks is directed at making them grow bigger. The more people you can make friends with and influence, the better it is for you – or so we are told. But is this necessarily true? The answer is 'not always' – for the following reasons:

- The bigger a network gets, the harder it is to control. Controlling networks (making them do what you want them to do) is a vital part of good networking practice – a subject we will be looking at later. A network that is out of control is dangerous and can turn round and deal you lethal blows.

- The dash for growth can sometimes lead to a relaxation of the selection standards – meaning you admit people who shouldn't really be there.

TIP

One way to grow your network is by putting some external dimensions onto it, ie seek to network with people other than your work colleagues (something you will find beneficial when, for example, you want to use networking to access jobs for you or as a source of information on conditions outside your own company). How do you do this? Join your appropriate professional body and go along to the meetings. Go on external courses. Attend conferences. See if there are any working parties or special interest groups you could join. Accept that this will mean giving up some of your own time.

15

- It adds to the (false) impression that networking is the preserve of social climbers and extrovert personality types. This can lead to a whole section of people feeling excluded.

Networks are best viewed as organic and not in need of any artificial growth stimulants. So, to a large extent, let the size of your network take care of itself. If you want to put more effort in anywhere, put it into making your existing network work for you and deliver the outcomes you are seeking to achieve.

GROWING NETWORKS AGAINST TARGETED CAREER AIMS

Whilst deprecating growth for growth's sake and trying to network with an ever-increasing number of people with no precise aim, we take quite a different view of getting onto networking terms with people who can influence career outcomes for you.

In our book *The Power of Networking* (also published by Kogan Page) we tell the story of the young apprentice who discovered his remote and rather ill-dispositioned managing director was addicted to the game of golf. With his eye to the main chance, the apprentice immediately bought himself a set of clubs and started taking lessons. Once proficient, the plan was to invite the managing director for a round one Saturday morning.

We never did hear how our apprentice got on but his story illustrates how there is a right and a wrong way of going about striking up a networking relationship with someone. Get it wrong and you could be putting yourself out of favour to the extent where the recipient of your networking overtures is frantically trying to work out how best to keep you at an arm's length. All the worse for you, of course, if the person concerned is someone whose influence could have a profound effect on the direction of your career.

THE BOND OF COMMON INTEREST AND SHARED EXPERIENCE

What any effective network has to have is a thread of common interest and/or shared experience – a bonding agent that will hold it together. In a family, for instance, the common interest is provided by the home, the family's economic well-being, the care of children and dependants, and so on. The shared experience, on the other hand, is to be found in family life: the high spots and the low spots, the coming through hardship together, the sharing of joy and sorrow.

With a professional network, the thread of common interest and/or shared experience is to be found in the work you do. Common interest, for example, will figure in the objectives of the organization to which you belong. If it is a commercial organization, maximizing the profit figure or seeing off competition will be items of common interest. As for shared experience, this could be pulling through a bad patch together or bringing a new product on stream.

The point to take in here is that there should be no need to invent pretexts for professional networking. The pretext is already there in the shape of your work. So what our young apprentice was seeking to do (have a networking relationship with the managing director based on the game of golf) was not really necessary. If his networking stood any chance of getting off the ground at all, the best basis for it was his and the managing director's shared experience of working together for the same organization.

PICKING THE RIGHT PEOPLE TO NETWORK WITH

In deciding who to bring into your networking circle you need first of all to define what you are seeking to achieve from your networking, ie your aims.

Aims vary enormously from one person to the next. For example, your aim could be trying to get a seat on the board of your company. Alternatively, it could be looking to make a complete change in the direction of your career. If you are thinking of going freelance, it could be seeking to get enough capital together to see you through your start-up period. With all of these aims there is usually someone somewhere who can influence the outcomes for you. This is not just the decision-makers themselves but people who have the ear of the decision-makers or people who are adept at pulling strings and moving behind the scenes.

GETTING THE NETWORK GOING

Having identified who you want to get onto networking terms with, the next question is how to get the ball rolling. At this point let's introduce Dean. Dean is going to tell you about how he started networking with someone who proved to be very useful to him:

Dean: I've been trying to get a posting to our Hong Kong office for almost two years and I have discussed this with my boss, Anna, on numerous occasions. Anna, for her part, simply seems to procrastinate and my worst fear is that she is doing this on purpose. The reason? My skills would be hard to replace and I wouldn't put it past Anna to put her own interests first. To add to my frustration, there have been several vacancies in the Hong Kong office recently and they have all been filled by outsiders.

I considered going over Anna's head and having a word with Gavin, the senior partner. This, I realized straight away, would be a high-risk game. One, Anna wouldn't like it and, two, Gavin being Gavin would be hesitant about doing anything that would undermine her.

OK, so it looks like Dean has fallen into the trap of being too useful (he wouldn't be the first!). But can networking help him? Let's find out:

Dean: Quite by chance I bumped into Florence on a trip to the vending machine. Like me, Florence started on the graduate training programme and she now works as a PA in the partners' office. We got talking and I told her about the problems I was having. She said she was sorry and promised to think of ways in which she could help.

Now let Florence take over the story:

Florence: I like Dean. He is a very positive person who is always prepared to give anyone a helping hand. In my own case, we had a panic in the office a few months back. Typical of Dean, he offered to stay behind and did the running up and down to the photocopier while I put the finishing touches to a huge report for a client that had to be ready for the couriers by 7 pm. As to Anna, good at her job she may be, but I could well believe her capable of putting obstacles in Dean's path.

I was sad to see Dean so down in the dumps and I rang him that same evening to say that I thought we ought to make Gavin aware of what was going on. At first Dean seemed reluctant. Guessing the reason, I told him I would make sure Gavin understood his concerns about going behind Anna's back.

Over to Gavin for the upshot:

Gavin: I was quite surprised to hear what Florence had to tell me about Dean. I had no idea he wanted to work in Hong Kong, though I could see straight away what a great asset he would be to the team in the Far East. What concerned me most though was that he should feel his career path was being blocked. We need committed young people like Dean and it would be a tragedy if he decided to leave. I was therefore very grateful to Florence for putting the word in my ear. We've got a retirement in Hong Kong coming up shortly, so what I'll do is go to Anna and tell her I think Dean is exactly the right person for the job. She'll gripe of course about having her staff taken off her, which will give me an opportunity to give her a lecture about never standing in the way of bright young people who want to get on.

Proof perhaps that to get where you want to get in life you occasionally have to pull a few strings. Not that Dean instigated this. The suggestion to pull strings came from Florence.

Key points to pick out from this case study are as follows:

- Quite unintentionally, Dean got himself onto networking terms with Florence by being helpful to her.

- The help was unsolicited.

- Because of her job Florence had the ear of the partners. She is therefore a good person to be on networking terms with.

TIP

If you want to strike up a networking relationship with someone, start by doing them a good turn. Little acts of help and kindness come few and far between in today's hustle-bustle world, so your gesture certainly won't go unnoticed. What you will be doing though is putting some inbound (reactive) traffic on your super-highway which will prepare the ground for when you want to send out the signals the other way.

One last, but very important point: the networking between Dean and Florence only worked because Dean projected a good image and it is interesting to speculate on what would have happened if this had not been the case. Would Florence have been quite so keen to take up his case with Gavin? Would she have stuck her neck out for him? Image and its importance in networking is what we will be looking at in the next chapter.

REVIEWING THE PERFORMANCE OF NEW MEMBERS OF YOUR NETWORK

As part of your good management of your network, put any new recruits on a trial period before you confer full membership rights on them. See how they perform the first few times you have occasion to network with them. Stand by to take action if you should find they don't come up to scratch.

ACTION NOTEPAD

- Identify any people you're networking with who could let you down. Take steps to remove them.

- Manage your network. Remember, as far as your network is concerned, it's you who's in charge (no one else).

- Don't put all your efforts into trying to network with more and more people. Give the time instead to making better use of your existing contacts (the benefits will be more immediate).

- Think through your aims. Identify any people who could help you achieve those aims.

- Find ways of getting onto networking terms with people who are in a position to pull strings for you. Help them if they need help. Feed them information where information would be useful to them.

2

PROJECTING THE RIGHT IMAGE

Why should anyone want to network with you? We ask this question not to fill you with self-doubt and paranoia but to get you to focus on the very real issue of image. How do you come across to people you know and how does the image you project affect your ability to network with them?

THE LIFELONG INTERVIEW

Imagine you've applied for a top job with a leading company and you're going along for your first interview. You'll be taking great pains over your appearance, of course. You'll probably rehearse a few good answers to the questions you're likely to be asked. You'll psych yourself up for the occasion and, when you're actually sitting in the hot seat, you'll be very careful not to say anything that could put you in a bad light. Indeed, if there are any grey areas in your track record, you'll be doing your best to draw a veil over them.

Not so though with people you come into contact with in the daily course of your work. You are less mindful of the image you project and, on occasions, you may even let a glimpse of one of the less endearing parts of your character slip out (we've all got a few of those!). Needless to say, the problem here is that we are talking about projecting an image day in day out rather than over the 45–60 minutes that's the norm for most job interviews. Harder? Of course it is and this is what we mean by the *lifelong interview*. It calls for a level of consistency and application that's not easy to achieve. It means for instance:

- You don't have off days.
- You have to be 100% reliable – you get back to people when you say you will.
- You complete your work to targets.
- Your appearance is always up to scratch (don't be the first to dress down!).
- You refrain from running down your colleagues and bosses behind their backs (keep your opinions to yourself).
- You don't whinge and whine (don't use your colleagues as sounding boards whenever you feel you're being given a hard time).
- You put the gloss you normally save up for job interviews into every day.

KEEPING YOUR FLAWS TO YOURSELF

One of the more difficult aspects of the lifelong interview to put into practice is learning to keep your flaws to yourself – difficult, because there's a natural tendency to form close relationships with people you meet through your work. Here's an example:

> *Tania:* The CEO called me into his office the other day and asked me if I knew anyone with the right experience to head up the new materials-handling division. My thoughts turned immediately to Graeme. Graeme and I worked together in my previous company and we know one another well. Graeme has exactly the right experience and, what's more, I happen to know he's not very happy with his job at the moment and anxious to make a move. Why did I hesitate about mentioning his name? Graeme had an alcohol problem about 10 years ago – something he told me in confidence. The problem, it seems, was brought on by pressure of work and resulted in him losing a senior management position with one of the market leaders in the industry. Getting the new division up and running isn't going to be any push-over, that's for certain, hence it bothered me that, put under pressure again, Graeme would go back on the bottle. I thought about it carefully and, after much soul-searching, I told the CEO that I couldn't think of anyone suitable.

Tania played safe and who can blame her? With anyone she recommends she will be putting her own reputation on the line, so giving Graeme a miss makes a lot of sense.

What's clear from this case study is that confiding to Tania cost Graeme the opportunity of a job (a job it sounds like he needed) and this illustrates how, contrary to popular belief, getting too close to someone in a professional networking relationship can be a mistake. The odd indiscretion or insight into some darker side of your personality

---

TIP

'It's who you know' used to be the catchphrase to describe how you got on in life. Today it's truer to say 'It's who you know and what they know about you'.

---

can slip out and, as in Graeme's case, the penalty will be in years to come. Exactly the same goes for letting your hair down in front of colleagues. What you did at the office party often comes back to haunt you.

The lesson? Always keep a careful control on the messages you feed out. In particular, beware of unintentionally using your network to disseminate damaging information (damaging to you, that is). Note: control is a key networking word and we shall be coming back to it time and time again.

ENSURING YOUR APPROACHABILITY

People have got to feel they are going to gain something from networking with you – emphasizing the importance of being receptive to the approaches that come zooming in on the inbound lane of your great superhighway. Being helpful and welcoming is therefore an important part of your image and one you need to cultivate. Conversely what you must never do is put the shutters up to anyone who networks with you either because you're too busy or because what they're asking you to do seems like a tall order. Instead always have the time of day for them. Always give them the impression that being on your network confers special privileges. In short, nothing should ever seem like too much trouble.

Easy? It should be, but to see how things can go wrong let's look at how Ali dealt with a call for help from Ruth.

Ali: She rang at about 8 o'clock one evening just as I was sitting down to eat a meal. She was putting the finishing touches to her CV and wanted to run it past me before sending it off in the post. Couldn't it wait? Ruth said no – the deadline for posting applications for the job she was interested in was the very next day. She wanted to fax it to me straight away.

Much as I like Ruth, I felt annoyed with her. She'd obviously left her CV till the last minute and I'd had a long, hard day. I ended up therefore telling her I couldn't help. I made the excuse I was meeting someone in town and was just on my way out when she rang.

The problem for Ali will be the next time she wants a favour from Ruth. When she does, she shouldn't be too surprised if she finds she gets a return dose of the cold shoulder treatment.

Lessons to be learned here are:

- Approachability frequently comes into conflict with the busy lives we all lead.

- Lack of approachability puts the kiss of death on networking. It kills off the traffic on the inbound lane.

- Being short or less helpful than we can be because one of our network contacts happens to catch us at a bad moment transmits an immediate signal which the person at the other end will be quick to pick up (be careful therefore about those long, drawn-out sighs!).

A point in passing here is that if the aim is to lose someone from your network (eg someone you no longer trust), then reversing your approachability and putting up the shutters should have the desired effect.

ACTION NOTEPAD

- Put on the gloss every day. Don't save your best image for interviews and special occasions.

- Control the messages you feed out about yourself. Don't use your networks to broadcast your flaws.

- Always have the time of day for your contacts. Give special priority to dealing with their needs.

- Do your best for your contacts. Let them see you are worth networking with.

3

GETTING THE
INFRASTRUCTURE
IN PLACE

As with any business, your network needs the right infrastructure to enable it to function properly, and in this
chapter we will be looking at the kind of things you need
to consider and, when you've got them, how to put them
to best use.

AVAILABILITY

First, let's look at availability. Availability is about providing
the wherewithal for your contacts to be able to reach you.
Availability goes hand in hand with approachability – the
subject we looked at in the last chapter. Approachability
and availability are what keeps the traffic on the inbound
lane of your great superhighway moving and what this
means is that you must make sure you're not putting any

obstacles in the paths of people who want to network with you. On the contrary, you need to be doing all in your powers to make it easy for them. The penalty for getting this wrong? You acquire the reputation of being one of those nightmare people who it's impossible to get to speak to. As a consequence, the people who're trying to network with you give up. The traffic on your inbound lane dwindles to a trickle and you're left wondering why.

Keeping your inbound lane clear is important for another reason. Some of the traffic on it will be in response to your *proactive* networking. So, for instance, if you've been putting the word round that you're looking for another job, some of the calls coming in could be from contacts who've come up with something interesting for you. Because of your lack of availability, however, you frustrate their attempts to get through and, as a consequence, you miss out on a chance. You are also making life difficult for them, meaning you score a bad point on your lifelong interview.

Approachability and availability are the twin pillars of good networking practice and you need to work on them. In particular you need to match your availability to your lifestyle and work patterns, and with the vast array of communication technology at your disposal today there is really no excuse for being hard to contact. Is there?

CHECKING OUT YOUR AVAILABILITY

If you're availability is bad, the chances are you'll be the last person to know about it. Here's an example:

Seb: I heard about an exciting business opportunity the other day. It consists of providing a large company with a complete recruitment and training package associated with the opening of one of their new distribution centres. But, whilst my organization has the expertise to do the recruitment, we don't have anyone who can handle operator training in warehouse skills up to acknowledged industry standards. It was here where my thoughts turned to Chas. Chas was the training manager in my last company up to when he was made redundant two months ago. I happen to

---

TIP

People who complain that no-one ever networks with them usually have their lack of availability to blame. So common is this problem that an *availability audit* is something we recommend to anyone aspiring to improve their networking skills. An availability audit means putting yourself in the position of someone trying to get hold of you. How easy would they find it? How would they get on if, for confidentiality reasons, they needed to speak to you at home in the evening? Would you be in? Would anyone be in? How many times would they find the number engaged? The idea of an availability audit is to throw up some points for action, such as, for example:

- Could you benefit from voice mail to take messages on your office phone extension?

- Is it time you got an answering machine at home or installed a second line?

- Do you need to introduce some domestic disciplines (like telling teenagers to spend less time on their calls)?

---

know Chas is looking for a stop-gap to tide him over while he finds another training manager's job – so this is why I thought he would be interested in doing a three-month contract for us. What happened when I tried to contact him at his home? The number rang out and there was no reply. I tried again in the evening only to find the line was permanently engaged. Puzzled, I didn't know what to do next. In the end my boss told me we'd have to forget Chas and find someone else to do the training. It was a pity really. Chas was by far the best man for the job.

Most failings in availability have pretty basic causes. In Chas's case he was spending his days brushing up on his IT skills at the local adult learning centre. In the evenings he was surfing the Internet, thus preventing any incoming calls from getting through. Chas was oblivious to the fact that Seb was trying to get hold of him. To this day he doesn't realize his lack of availability cost him a lucrative contract with Seb's firm (and the handy cash that went with it).

INVESTING IN AVAILABILITY

With the advent of mobile phones, tele-messaging, com-bined phones, faxes and answering machines, e-mail, features on standard phones such as call diversion and call-waiting signals, phone companies offering one number contactability etc, there is clearly a lot out there for budding networkers to spend their money on.

Will it help you? The answer to this question is it depends a lot on your life patterns. For example, if you work nine to five and spend most evenings at home, you shouldn't present too many challenges to someone wanting to get hold of you. If you work erratic hours, however, or if you travel a lot on business, investment in communications technology is clearly going to enhance your ability to network with people tremendously. Here, working out your own solutions is part of the fun – and remember that availability is something you should always be striving to perfect. Keep your eyes open therefore for 'anything new' on the market. This is a field in which things are changing almost daily.

BROADCASTING YOUR AVAILABILITY

Irrespective of how much you spend on the infrastructure of your professional network, it won't do you a lot of good if no one knows about it. People you network with need to have the following information:

- your home and work addresses and telephone numbers;

- the number of your mobile phone;

- your e-mail address (if you have one);

- any other way of contacting you (eg do you have a fax machine at home? If so, what number do users dial to access it?).

A good place to put all this information is on a personal business card, which you can either produce yourself on your own PC or ask the local print shop to produce for you (either way, it's not going to cost you a lot). Here is an example:

Stephanie Judd
Judd Computer Services, 1 Main Street,
Anytown AT1 X99
Phone: Office: 333 333 333
        Home: 555 555 555
        Mobile: 888 888 888
e-mail: stephaniejudd@xx.co.uk

Having your phone numbers listed and identified as home, office, mobile, etc alongside your e-mail address and/or your private fax number gives your contacts all the information they need in one place if they have to get hold of you in a hurry for any reason. Remember to advise your contacts if your numbers should change, eg because you move jobs. What's the best way to do this? By having a new card printed and sending it out with instructions to destroy the old one. (See also what we've got to say about mailshots a few pages on.)

USING YOUR AVAILABILITY CORRECTLY

How your networking benefits from investment in technology also depends on how disciplined you are in the way you use it.

A common problem here is people who don't check their answering machines. The same goes for people who don't look at their e-mails regularly. Sadly, failing to respond to a contact in an acceptable period of time (worse still, failing to respond at all) sends out an immediate negative message. You don't rate the person as important enough to break into your daily routines – or that's the way it seems. Even if apologies are accepted, the fact you don't check your messaging devices systematically won't do you a lot of good on the lifelong interview front.

What if your lifestyle and/or work patterns make it difficult for you to check faxes and e-mails regularly? Our answer would be don't use them or at least don't advertise their existence as far as your network contacts are concerned.

WHAT TO DO IF YOU FIND NO ONE IS NETWORKING WITH YOU

Go through this short checklist and see if you can put your finger on the problem. Doing this will also act as a fail-safe to make sure you've taken in all that we've covered so far.

● Are you trying to network with people with whom you have no common interest/shared experience? If so, stop and think again.

● Are you spreading your net sufficiently by joining professional bodies and using other opportunities to meet people outside your own firm? If not, start today by identifying three ways in which you could do this. Devise a plan and then decide how your are going to put it into effect.

● How do you measure up as far as projecting the work-perfect and person-perfect image goes? If you suspect your image may be slightly tarnished, start today on getting it right. Your networking will benefit from turning over a new leaf.

● Are you responding correctly to people trying to network with you? Are you being as helpful as you can be? A sign that your approachability is going wrong is when people don't come back.

● Are you getting too close to people you meet through

35

the course of your work? Are you revealing aspects of your character that you should really be keeping to yourself? If so, learn from your mistakes and make sure in future you control the messages you feed out about yourself.

- Is it difficult to get hold of you? Have you tried doing an availability audit, and if so, what was the result? If availability is your problem, take urgent steps to do something about it.

- Is your availability sufficiently advertised? Are the people you would like to network with aware of how to get hold of you? If not, follow the advice in this chapter.

- Are you rigorous about reading your e-mails regularly and checking the messages on your answering machine? Are you equally rigorous about getting back to people who have left messages?

If you can honestly put a tick alongside each of these bullet points, then you are well on your way to becoming a good networker. Have patience and your effort will pay off.

KEEPING DETAILS OF YOUR NETWORK CONTACTS

Back to infrastructure. If you haven't already got it, something you need is a place to keep details of all your network contacts, including details of how to get hold of them. An address book or a personal organizer immediately springs to mind and this satisfies one important criterion: you need your contact file to be in portable form so you can have it to hand at all times. Portability, however, invites the possibility of loss, so always keep a back-up copy of your contact file, eg a card system that you keep at home or, perhaps better still, a file stored on disk.

MAILSHOTTING YOUR NETWORK

Why is your contact file better stored on disk? For the simple reason that it facilitates what we want to talk about next.

From time to time you will need to communicate with your contacts, eg to advise them of a new telephone number or if you change jobs. If your IT skills are up to it, the easiest way to do this is by using the mailmerge facility on your PC software to produce a set of personalized letters. As well as communicating the information you need to communicate, these will look good (good for your person-perfect image) and remind everyone in a very visible form that you're still there (the fact that networks occasionally need a little nudge to keep the two-way traffic flowing is a subject we will be touching on in the next chapter).

What about really stepping up a gear and producing an occasional newsletter for your contacts? A bit like a company house journal except the news will be all about you? We must confess to having reservations about newsletters, especially the sort that degenerate into toe-curling yarns about what people get up to at the weekends or what they've been doing with the kids. Our advice? Don't do it unless you've got something to say that's (a) interesting and (b) connected with your work, eg if you've been on a business trip overseas. Remember we're talking about professional networking here.

CREATING SPACE
FOR YOURSELF

Is there anything else you need in the way of infrastructure?

Because of its very nature, a lot of networking is carried on from home. Either it's easier to get hold of contacts in the evening or the subject matter you want to talk about is not for the ears of people in the office. This begs the question: do you have anywhere sufficiently private at home and free from distracting background noises (eg barking dogs or the sound of a television)? If the answer is no, then take steps to create a bit of space for yourself. At the very minimum this means an extension off your phone into a quiet room. Better still is if you use a room at home as an office. Here is where you could install a separate phone/fax/e-mail line with 'hands off' instructions as far as other members of your family are concerned.

VIEW YOUR NETWORKING
AS IMPORTANT

This underlies everything we've had to say about infrastructure. Networks – your cultivation of them and the way you use them – can have a significant bearing on the progress of your career. So don't neglect them by under-resourcing them. Instead give them the proper respect they deserve and you'll find that when you have a need for them, they'll be there, waiting to serve you.

ACTION NOTEPAD

- Pay attention to your approachability and availability. Make sure you are easy to deal with.

- Let people see they've got something to gain from networking with you. Do your best for them. Let them see you as a person who gets results.

- Take stock of your work patterns and domestic routines. Identify where modern communications technology could help improve your availability. Invest accordingly.

- Make sure your contacts know how to get hold of you.

- Make sure your availability works. Make sure you're not the cause of your own problems by failing to check e-mails and message-taking devices regularly and routinely.

4

GETTING YOUR NETWORKS TO PERFORM EFFECTIVELY

'Perform' in this context means perform for **you**.

Having your very own professional network at your disposal is no use to you at all unless it is capable of delivering the outcomes you are seeking to achieve. Here is where the fine-tuning comes in: recognizing the tremendous power of networking and channelling it in directions you want it to go in, or, if you like, taming the beast and making it respond to your instructions.

SMALL WORLDS

There is an inherent problem in networking and it is this. It will only ever access small worlds for you and this, in turn, reflects:

- the number of people who will pass the selection test for your network will never be that many;

- the geographical areas in which you work;

- the profession/trade/line of business in which you are engaged.

Outside these small worlds the power of your networking diminishes significantly. For instance, your professional network will probably not be a lot of help to you if you want to move into a completely different career.

A corollary of these small worlds is that they are often quite tightly knit – meaning there is a lot of potential for information you share with network contacts reaching other ears, including the wrong ones. Here is an example:

> *Marcia:* I put in an application to XYZ Industries, who happen to be one of our biggest competitors. One of my colleagues, Brett, used to work for XYZ Industries so I had a quiet word with him to see if I could get some inside information on the way they operate. Brett was very helpful and gave me lots of useful low-down. But what I didn't bargain for was that Brett would tell Lester that I was thinking of going to work for XYZ and Lester being Lester spilt the beans to Ann, my boss. The result was a very heated discussion in which Ann came very close to telling me to collect my cards (like the rest of our top management team there is no love lost between Ann and XYZ!).

Office tittle-tattle maybe, but, as far as Marcia is concerned, the damage is done – damage in terms of damage to her relationship with her boss, Ann and, through Ann, with the rest of the top brass in her company. What went wrong of course was the failing on Marcia's part to instil into Brett the need for strictest confidence. Crystal-clear instructions should have been given to him not to discuss the matter with anyone else, together with the reason.

KEEPING YOUR NETWORKS UNDER CONTROL

A network that is out of control is a network that won't serve you well and, as in Marcia's case, it is one that could let you down very badly indeed. The lesson? With pro-active networking the messages you feed out to your contacts need to be very precise and defined. Notably they should be **complete** messages, meaning:

● If the subject matter is confidential, they should include instructions not to discuss the matter with anyone except yourself – and the reason why.

● You should define in exact terms what you want your contact to do for you – this is to prevent them doing something else, either because they don't understand where you're coming from or because they think they're helping you (usually they're not!).

● You should set out any time parameters, so if, for example, you need some information by next week, your contact is fully aware of the fact.

● If you want your contact to report back to you at certain points, you should make this absolutely clear – for example, if you're using your contact to access a job opportunity, you may want him or her to find out the salary first, ie before you decide whether to put in an application.

TAPPING INTO OTHER PEOPLE'S NETWORKS

No-one in the world is more than six phone calls away and this tantalizing prospect has served to inspire a whole generation of budding networkers! Sadly, however, the reality is rather different, but before we start pouring too much cold water on claims that you can network with practically anyone, let's take a closer look at what happens when you have dealings with contacts second- and third-hand. More to the point, let's identify the snags, then see what we can do to iron some of them out. In short, let's see what we can do to make extended networking of this kind work for you.

Back to basics first. Everyone has a network – a network that is different to everyone else's. This means that people you network with will have networks that are different to yours. Some of the people will be the same because you have moved in similar circles, but some won't, and, with extended networking in mind, it is this latter group that we need to be focusing on. On closer inspection, however, we find that these contacts of contacts divide into three sub-groups:

- **first**, people you know but who you choose not to network with (for example, people you find unsatisfactory or untrustworthy);

- **second**, people you know and who you have nothing against but who you are not on networking terms with;

- **third**, people you don't know.

The first sub-group we can, of course, put to one side straight away. Now let's look at one of the big problems of networking through intermediaries: the control you need to have over what's going on has to be exercised by others and, needless to say, the further you go down one of these networking chains, the harder the control becomes. As a consequence the kind of dangers we looked at a few pages back start to rear their ugly heads. The wrong ears could pick up the fact you're on the look out for another job. Your aims could be misinterpreted and you could find yourself being steered onto a course you don't want to follow. All sorts of things can happen.

How can you avoid this? One option open to you is to forge a direct link with your contact's contacts, ie bring them onto your network and under your own (better) control. With the second of the three sub-groups (individuals you know and who are acceptable to you) networking direct instead of by proxy is an avenue you could certainly explore.

But what about the last group (the people you don't know). Here you are left with two choices: either you ask your contact to effect an introduction with a view to striking up a direct networking relationship, or you trust your contact to exercise the control for you, ie you delegate the task but with clear terms of reference.

With networking down a chain, however, a dilemma can and often does arise. A further case study will help to illustrate this.

Sam: I saw a job advertised in the newspaper the other day that sounded right up my street. Everything seemed right: the salary, the location, the prospects for further training – the only snag was the company was one I'd never heard of before. Who could I turn to for information? My immediate thought was Amrik. It turned out, however, that Amrik was little the wiser than me, though he said he knew someone who he thought could help. Half an hour later Amrik rang me back. He said he'd spoken to his contact but the feedback wasn't very good. The company had the reputation of being a hire and fire organization with a high turnover of staff and the advice was to steer well clear.

The dilemma for Sam is whether to proceed with his application or not. The problem is he doesn't know Amrik's contact, so he doesn't know how much faith to put in the information he's been given. What should he do next?

Where the subject of the networking could have important consequences for you (as in Sam's case) a sensible step to take is to seek corroboration of any information that has come to you down a chain (irrespective of whether it conforms with what you want to hear or not). You can do this by tapping into more than one source, ie ring round a few more of your contacts.

WARNING!

Networking with people you don't know is potentially dangerous. Don't do it unless you have to. Even then, exert as much control over what's going on as you possibly can.

KNOWING WHEN TO TAKE MATTERS INTO YOUR OWN HANDS

Networking is great at opening doors but there comes a point (always) when it is best for you to start dealing direct. Take networking for a job as an example. A contact may be great at doing the sounding out for you and effecting the introductions, but when it gets to the nitty-gritty like defining the responsibilities or negotiating the pay, this is best done by you. Why? Misunderstanding creeps in, nuances get missed, all sorts of things can happen which could go on to have a bearing on your future.

For this reason it is important to define at the outset what you expect your networking to achieve for you. When that aim has been met, it's time for your contact to step aside and let you take over. Note: part of keeping control is telling your contacts how far you want them to go.

KEEPING THE TWO-WAY TRAFFIC FLOWING

A common experience is to find you have a need for networking then discover your network is no longer there. The name of your contact in ABC Industries has slipped your memory; Jo who worked for DEF & Associates has moved on (no-one can recall where); Tim's number is no longer in the phone book, and you're worried about ringing Charlie simply because it's been such a long time since the two of you last spoke.

What this emphasizes is that networks thrive on use. The more traffic there is whizzing backwards and forwards, the more effectively your network will perform for you or – to put it another way – networking doesn't benefit from the stop–start treatment. It needs to be ongoing.

How do you achieve this? One way we've looked at already – by taking out the obstacles and ensuring that your approachability and availability works at all times. But this doesn't take away the fact that you may not have a need to speak to certain individuals on a very regular basis. What then? The answer is that this is where a bit of cheating comes in. Ring them on an invented pretext. You need a second opinion on something or there could be some interesting information on a mutual acquaintance that you thought to pass on – the subject almost doesn't matter. The fact that you're there on the end of the phone is all that counts. It serves not just as a reminder of your existence but also of your approachability and availability. Any feeling of awkwardness that surrounds relationships with people you haven't spoken to for a long time will automatically be taken away.

Of course, inventing a pretext won't be necessary if you've got some genuine reason for ringing up – like you've moved jobs or your phone number has changed.

TIP

Run through your list of contacts from time to time and ask yourself when you last spoke to them. If 12 months or more have lapsed then take the emergency resuscitation action described above. Failing to do this could mean a link of your network falls into disuse. When you need it, it won't be there.

ACTION NOTEPAD

- Identify what you want your networking to achieve (a clear aim).

- Control the messages you feed out. Make sure they're consistent with the aim.

- Don't use your contacts as a sounding board for your grouses and groans. It communicates no precise aim and there is danger of you being misunderstood.

- Tell your contacts exactly what you expect of them. Don't leave them to make their own interpretations.

- Where confidentiality is of the essence always impress this on your contacts. Explain the reasons.

- Don't delegate to your contacts the jobs you should be doing yourself. Use them to open doors, but once you're through them, take over.

- Keep in touch with your contacts. Don't let your network die from neglect.

5

APPLYING YOUR NETWORKING SKILLS

So far we have been concentrating on bringing you up to speed in the four core skills that are the underpinnings to all effective networking. To recap these are:

- picking the right people to network with;

- putting yourself across to these people in the best possible light;

- controlling the messages you feed out to them;

- responding to the messages they feed to you.

Given that you constantly strive to perfect these skills, the two-way traffic on your networking superhighway will keep flowing. You will have a powerful force at your fingertips and all you will have to do is unleash it when you need it and stand by for the results.

GETTING YOUR CAREER BREAKS
BY NETWORKING

If you're newly qualified or if you're seeking to make a change in your career, the power of networking can help you to get the breaks. How? The answer is in two ways.

The first is by using your network as a source of advice on career choices. For example, if you're toying with the idea of becoming a doctor, do you know anyone who is a doctor? Alternatively, do any of your contacts know anyone who is a doctor? You will find first-hand information straight from the horse's mouth very useful to you when faced with important decisions such as these.

The second is by networking your way into your first career job (because of your lack of experience, this could be one of the toughest hurdles you ever have to face). Here you need someone to effect an introduction for you, a contact who can put a word in the right ears – for example, someone who already works for the organization you wish to join. Where competition for jobs is intense – as it often is with career starts – using your network to effect an introduction is a way of making sure you stand out from the crowd. Put simply, if the string is there, make sure you pull it.

WARNING!

Back to ensuring you always pick the right people to network with. If your introduction is effected by someone who is held in high esteem by an employer, it will go a long way towards smoothing your path to getting the job. On the other hand, if the person who introduces you is viewed as ineffective or lazy, you will, by association, be tarred with the same brush.

Your success in your new job (and how long you last in it!) will depend to a large extent on the links you forge with your bosses and the people you work with. Your lifelong interview obviously has a big part to play in this (keeping your image squeaky clean), but, at the same time, always

---

TIP

Getting starts in life can be very tough, especially at the beginning of your career when your professional network is at its smallest and least able to help (consisting perhaps of just a handful of contacts from university or the jobs you did during your holidays). So how do you go about getting your foot in the door when you don't actually know anyone on the inside?

The answer is the 'Trojan Horse Technique' – the reason for the name will become apparent shortly.

Whilst career-start jobs may be very thin on the ground, especially in times of economic recession, what is always in relatively abundant supply is low-grade, low-skill work, much of it temporary and/or part time. The trick is to worm your way into organizations in one of these lowly capacities then attack them from the inside – rather like the Greeks did at the Battle of Troy. Your weapon, in this instance, will be the power of your networking. Your presence in an organization will enable you to forge links with people at all levels – something that would not be possible for you to do from the outside.

Note: There's a lot more about the Trojan Horse Technique and its application in our book *The Power of Networking* (Kogan Page, 1999). It can be used in any situation where getting your foot in the door is difficult.

---

have special regard for people who can influence outcomes for you or who you depend on for advice and guidance (people who could tip the scales for you as far as your success or failure is concerned). Remember the tip about those little acts of kindness (the case study of Dean and Florence on pages 18–20). Doing the fetching and carrying for someone or making a cup of coffee for them when they're busy can go a very long way.

USING YOUR NETWORKS TO ACCESS PROMOTION

This is where you need to focus on one of your more important professional relationships – the relationship between you and your boss. Your boss will figure largely in any decisions about your future, so your chances of promotion will be greatly enhanced by any favourable impressions you manage to make – which brings us back again to the life-long interview and the importance of projecting a person-perfect and work-perfect image every day. But to see how this works in practice – and to draw out a few further lessons – let's take a look at another case study. This time the tale is told by Charles, the chief executive of a large manufacturing company.

Charles: A few months ago I had the job of picking a successor for the Operations Director who retires in six months. What I needed for this position was a good team leader, someone who would inspire confidence in the workforce and, at the same, introduce some discipline. Out of all the talent available, why did I go for John? For the simple reason that I had the good fortune to work for him when I first joined the company as a graduate trainee 15 years ago (he was a section head at the time). What I liked most about John was the way he always led by example, setting high standards both for himself and for his subordinates, correcting where necessary and never forgetting to give praise where praise was due. It was John I had to thank for my first big break with the company. He put my name forward to manage the project when we brought our first completely computerized production line on stream. He was also there to offer any advice – and came to my rescue a few times when I rubbed the factory management team up the wrong way!

I think John will make an excellent operations director. It's a promotion he certainly deserves.

The points to pick out from this case study are as follows:

- John made an excellent job of his lifelong interview. He maximized any benefits from his long-standing relationship with the upwardly mobile Charles.

- Charles was once John's subordinate – illustrating how your lifelong interview always needs to have a 360 degree orientation to it.

- Evidence of having a good networking relationship with your boss is when he or she is actively looking after your best interests and ensuring that your ambitions are fulfilled.

YOUR NETWORK AS A SOURCE OF INFORMATION

We have touched on this briefly already. Your contacts can act as a source of information and this can work for you in two ways. In the first scenario, you need to know something (eg the low-down on a company you are thinking of

55

joining), so you ring round your professional network to see if anyone can help. In the second, one of your contacts hears of something that would be beneficial for you to know, so they ring you.

> *Karen:* I found out that my company was up for sale from an outside contact who overheard a conversation in a hotel where she was staying. This enabled me to start getting some irons in the fire quickly and, as a result, I had two job offers in my hand when the announcement was made that we'd been taken over by the biggest bunch of sharks in the industry!

Information fed to you through your network is often information that would be difficult or impossible for you to access by any other means. To have a source like this at your fingertips is, therefore, one of the many bonuses you will get from improving your networking skills.

NETWORKING FOR JOBS

Does it surprise you to learn that 50 per cent of jobs are filled by networking and even higher figures have been quoted for top-drawer jobs? What this points to is the ever-increasing importance of the so-called 'invisible job market' – the jobs that are never advertised; the jobs that are hard to find out about; the jobs that are often the best jobs.

So how can you access jobs like these? How will your improved networking skills help you to penetrate the mysterious world of the invisible job market? Jobs can be sourced by both proactive and reactive networking. Here's how:

Proactive. Ringing round contacts who work for other employers to see if they know of anything suitable for you. If so, getting your contacts to effect the introductions. (This kind of activity has a habit of being sparked off by an event – such as being made redundant or getting a poor pay increase.)

Reactive. Receiving unsolicited approaches either direct from contacts or through intermediaries (including consultants).

How successful you are at sourcing jobs by proactive and reactive networking depends largely on how successful you have been at projecting the right image through the medium of your lifelong interview. For instance, if Jack asks Jill to help by finding him a job with her firm, Jill will want to feel pretty sure about him before she proceeds. Similarly, if Jill is asked by her principals to suggest someone who might be suitable for a job, she needs to feel very confident about Jack before putting his name forward.

GETTING HEADHUNTED

Headhunting has given reactive networking a further and very exciting dimension. Headhunters operate at the very top end of the job market, so an approach from one is a pretty sure sign you're on your way up (that's the exciting part).

How do headhunters work? The answer is that they thrive on their contacts in the business world – contacts they take great pains to cultivate. So, whenever one of their clients comes up with a recruitment need, the headhunters ring round their network of contacts to see if anyone can provide the names of suitable candidates (candidates the headhunters then approach). Where this works for you is where your networking skills have brought you into contact with someone who is on a headhunter's list of telephone numbers. This is how you end up getting those mysterious telephone calls from people you've never heard of before.

Important: Headhunters sell themselves by reputation, hence the very last thing any of them want is to place a candidate with a client who subsequently turns out to be a duffer. With future billings at stake they play safe (always). So don't expect to be headhunted for a top job until you have mastered your lifelong interview skills and managed to project a person-perfect and work-perfect image to those who you network with.

USING YOUR NETWORK TO SOURCE BUSINESS

Contacts are lifeblood as far as people in sales are concerned. Contacts form a major part of marketing their skills to prospective employers.

But, with the increasing number of people who work in one-man/one-woman businesses or other small enterprises, professional networking as a source of business has assumed a wider importance.

First, a fairly typical experience:

> *Stella:* I'm a graphic designer and I went freelance a couple of years ago because I saw it as a way of making more money. I put a mailshot round the trade advertising my services but found, much to my surprise, it yielded practically zilch. Where does my business come from today? The answer is the advertising agency where I used to work – plus a few clients who came to me by recommendation.

Like many others, Stella has discovered it's far easier to get work where your face is known. Lifelong interview in action again? Yes, you've got it right in one, but here's another piece of advice to bear in mind:

TIP

For people who're in business on their own account, an important source of work is often their previous employers. It is vital therefore always to leave jobs on good terms. So don't, whatever you do, see handing in your resignation as the opportunity to get a few long-standing grouses off your chest or harangue the boss with a list of home truths. Instead bite your tongue, complete any outstanding work to the very best of your ability and leave with your person-perfect and work-perfect image fully intact.

GOING INTO BUSINESS WITH PEOPLE YOU NETWORK WITH

For those concerned, choosing someone to go into business with is a very important decision. **Get it right** and you could go on to do great things together. **Get it wrong** and your business partnership could become the business partnership from hell.

Choosing a business partner from among the circle of people you network with professionally has many advantages:

- You'll be looking at people you know and, because you network with them, they will be people who have come up to standard as far as your selection test is concerned.

- The bond of common interest and shared experience ensures like-mindedness as far as matters of principle are concerned (absence of like-mindedness on matters of principle is a common reason for people in partnerships falling out).

59

● The bonding agent will also be there to enable you to transcend the bickering and minor disagreements that are a normal part of life in any small business enterprise. The business is ensured a life that goes on after the strife.

TIP

Short of actually going into business together, people in networking relationships often have the capacity to combine their talents for mutual profit. For example, if you are a builder and if you network with someone who is an architectural technician, you can team up together to offer one of your clients a complete design and build package. At the end you split the proceeds then go your separate ways – until the next need arises, that is.

ACTION NOTEPAD

● Make your network work for you. Don't be afraid to use it. The more traffic on it, the better it performs.

● Get your career breaks by networking. Find the back ways into organizations that are difficult to penetrate.

● When it comes to projecting a person-perfect and work-perfect image, don't forget your peers and subordinates. Remember, networks are for life and, in years to come, peers and subordinates could be in positions to influence important outcomes for you.

● Share information with your network contacts. Tell them if you hear anything that's potentially useful to them. Reap the benefit of having information passed back to you in return.

- Turn to your network in moments of need. If you're made redundant, for example, get your contacts to see what employment opportunities they can unearth for you. The same goes when your career is in a rut and going nowhere.

- Networking is your way into the elusive invisible job market. Take special note if you're aspiring to jobs at the top of the tree. Work on your person-perfect and work-perfect image to enhance your chances of receiving approaches from headhunters.

- If your livelihood depends on sourcing business, see your network as there to help you. As a general rule, people who network with you will be happy to give you work. Remember to do the same for them if the positions are ever reversed.

- If you work freelance or as part of a small enterprise, identify opportunities for teaming up with networking contacts and profiting from combined effort.

Do you want to learn more about professional networking?

Our book *The Power of Networking* is available from all leading bookshops or by visiting the Kogan Page Web site at www.kogan-page.co.uk. Alternatively, you can e-mail orders to: orders@kogan-page.co.uk.

6

DOS AND DON'TS OF EFFECTIVE NETWORKING

DO:

- network with people who can influence positive outcomes for you;
- put effort into projecting a person-perfect and work-perfect image at all times;
- have the time of day for your network contacts;
- advise your contacts if your phone number changes or you move jobs;
- check your messages and e-mails regularly and consistently;
- get back to people when you say you will;
- make sure your contacts know what you expect from them;

- use your networks;
- leave jobs on good terms.

DON'T:

- network with people you don't know;
- network with people who could let you down;
- try to network with people with whom you've got no common interest or shared experience;
- let people you work with in on your darker secrets (keep them to yourself);
- use your network for gossip and spreading rumours;
- lose touch with contacts;
- miss opportunities for using your networking skills.